AF264615

CHERRY St. FACTORY (Court Yard View)

COLUMBIA AVENUE & 5TH ST. FACTORY.

DESCRIPTION

OF THE

Establishment

OF

CORNELIUS & BAKER,

MANUFACTURERS OF

Lamps, Chandeliers & Gas Fixtures,

PHILADELPHIA.

———————

MANUFACTORIES:
CHERRY STREET, BETWEEN EIGHTH AND NINTH,
AND
COLUMBIA AVENUE AND FIFTH STREET.

WARE-ROOMS:
No. 710 CHESTNUT STREET.

———————

PHILADELPHIA:
J. B. CHANDLER, PRINTER, 306 CHESTNUT STREET, [GIRARD BUILDING.]

The following description was published in one of our city papers.

Having had frequent calls from our friends for the account, we have concluded to arrange it in this form, as being most suitable for preservation.

CORNELIUS & BAKER,
PHILADELPHIA.

Lamps, Chandeliers and Gas Fixtures.

There are scarcely any articles of utility or ornament
which are of more remote antiquity than lamps. They
are spoken of and critically described in the Old Testa-
ment. Two thousand, three hundred and fifty years
ago Moses prescribed the form for the seven branched
chandelier which was to be placed in the Jewish Taber-
nacle.

Lamps of different shapes were found among the
ruins of Pompeii and Herculaneum. The parable of
the wise and foolish virgins, uttered nearly nineteen
hundred years ago, is familiar to every one. Time out
of date the Chinese have used myriads of lamps and
lanterns in their jubilees, funerals, and in fact, on all
other important occasions. The primitive Christians
used a great profusion of lamps in their religious cere-
monies, while to this day both the Jews and the Catho-
lics keep lamps constantly burning before their altars.
These facts not only prove the high antiquity of the
articles in question, but exhibit the Jew and the Gen-
tile, the Christian and the Heathen, from the earliest
dawning of the arts instinctively obeying the first great
Divine command, " Let there be light !"

The Safety Lamp, which protects the poor miner from explosions of choke-damp, has immortalized the name of Sir Humphry Davy, its inventor.   Light houses have guided many a tempest-tossed mariner to a haven of safety, or warned him of hidden dangers; while the " midnight lamp" seems to be considered, by sentimental people, the only article of any use to hard-working students.   The word "lamp" is derived from a Greek word which signifies to shine.   The article itself is not only of great practical utility, but it has from time immemorial furnished figures and themes for poets, and symbols for almost all classes of worshippers.

The ancients endeavored to obtain a lamp which should burn eternally without the necessity of being replenished with oil.   This desideratum was sought after as eagerly as the philosopher's stone, or the perpetual motion of later days, and with about as much success.

Quite a number of works have been written upon this subject; some of their authors asserting that the thing was possible, and pretending to believe that tombs had been opened in which these unquenchable lamps were found burning.   The object of the eternal lamp was to chase away the spirits which could only flourish in the dark.   Scott, in the " The Lay of the Last Minstrel," describes such a lamp in the sepulchre of the wizard, Michael Scott, in Melrose Abbey. Sir Walter admitted, however, that it was a poetic fiction. One of these perpetual lamps is said to have been found burning in the tomb of Tullia, the daughter of Cicero. The wick was supposed to be composed of asbestos, which was doubtless more expensive than the cotton article. Kircher enumerates three different methods for constructing such a lamp, but wisely concludes by saying, that the thing is nevertheless impossible. Various old authors believed such utensils could be made, and considered them as coming within the province of natural magic, which art at the present day is considered exploded.

We have lately visited Cornelius & Baker's celebrated manufactory of lamps and chandeliers, and have taken some pains to make ourselves familiar with the mysteries of art necessary to transform shapeless masses of copper and spelter, into magnificent chandeliers, beautiful candelabras, neat gas fixtures, and the world of tasteful affairs which are designed to ornament and illuminate palace, hall, church, theatre, or private parlor.

Prior to the establishment of this house the manufacture of lamps in Philadelphia was a very unimportant branch of the industry of the city. A few hands were employed in working at such common articles as were necessary for ordinary domestic uses. Churches and theatres were generally illuminated by means of candles. The beaux and belles of that day danced in ball rooms lighted by candles or smoky oil lamps. The next day there was usually a scraping off of grease or wax from coats and dresses. These accidents were then considered inevitable results of the night's festivity. Chandeliers in those days were very rare, and only imported at an extravagant cost. The introduction of gas, important improvement in machinery, and the spirit of private enterprise, have effected a great revolution. Now chandeliers have become articles of general use.

About fifty years ago the founder of the present firm of Cornelius & Baker commenced business with two or three journeymen. As his trade increased, the original workshop became too small, and an adjoining house was added to the concern. This was soon too much crowded; the demand increased; more room was required, house after house was absorbed until a fourth part of a square was devoted to turning metals into all conceivable shapes. On the night of the 12th of December, 1854, one of the buildings caught fire, and before the flames could be arrested all were destroyed, fortunately most of the patterns were in another factory erected in a different part of the city so that the loss was not as heavy as it might have been. This firm immediately set to work to put up a building that would be entirely fire-proof and they have well succeeded, not a pound of nails nor a particle of wood was used in the construction of the building, it is all composed of brick and iron, built in the form of a hollow square, five stories high; the floors are of brick, the stairs and window sash of iron, and the roof of slate and iron, it was the first fire-proof building erected in the city, and presents quite a beautiful and striking appearance from the outside. Several hundred men, aided by a large steam-engine form the great motive power of this busy hive. Let us go in and see.

There is a great variety in the character of the labor bestowed on articles manufactured here. Every grade of workman, from the common laborer to the artist and chemist is engaged. We must strive to avoid confusion, and will endeavor so to arrange our plan of examination as to be able to convey to the reader an adequate idea of the numerous processes necessary in the manufacture of the various articles we have before spoken of.

We will first enter one of the modeling rooms. Each

modeler has a private room. Here all the patterns for the castings are made. The operator is an artist, and upon his skill the beauty of form and design depends. A glance is sufficient to assure us we are in a studio. The walls are covered with drawings and sketches of almost every object; things of the most fantastical shapes; specimens of the beautiful in all the kingdoms of nature and in every department of art; contributions have been levied from earth, air and sea, and an encyclopedia calculated to gratify taste or caprice is the result. Here knights in armor, and clowns in motley guise, flourish in most loving companionship with birds, beasts and fishes. There a waxen Wellington and a plaster Napoleon lay "cheek by jole." Here are specimens of Egyptian, Doric, Ionic, Corinthian and Gothic architecture, and natural and artificial flowers, singly and in groups. These combined make up a rare collection of beautiful pieces, which suggest to the modeler and guide him in the production of his designs.

Our artist has before him a mass of prepared wax. A portion of this plastic material is laid upon a thin board. He then proceeds to mould it rudely into shape with his fingers, governing himself by a sketch which is placed before him. After the design is "roughed out," he consummates his task with the aid of instruments made of hard wood. When the pattern—which is frequently the work of weeks—is finally completed, it goes into the hands of the caster, who makes a mould of it in brass, which is sent to the "chaser," and finally finished and elaborated into the dignity of a standard pattern, from which the caster may multiply an infinity of copies. It is a very nice operation to make a mould from the original wax pattern; the fragile material of which it is composed renders it imperatively necessary to use every precaution in obtaining a brazen fac-simile of the original.

Much depends upon the skill and taste of the "chaser." When the first copy of the original pattern is placed in his hands, the embellishments on its surface are faint and require to be deepened. Many of its distinctive features are to be given it by him. The partially developed fibres and veins of leaves and flowers, the feathers of birds and the fur of animals, have to be defined or made more distinct. The operator here uses steel instruments, somewhat resembling small chisels; these tools have various shapes, with which the necessary indentations are made by sharp blows with a light hammer. When the embellishments are thus perfected, and all the objectionable inequalities removed, the pattern is considered complete, and it is ready to go into the hands of the caster.

It must be remembered that, where the design has certain curves and bends, the caster could not, without much trouble, make a mould from it if the pattern was given into his hands in that form. It is, therefore, found easier and more expeditious to flatten the pattern. For instance, if a drooping feather, or a crumpled vine leaf were to be cast, the pattern would be formed so as to present a flat surface. After the casting is finished, the proper bends are given to it by means of wooden mallets and other tools. This plan obviates the necessity of a "core."

Having finished with this branch of our subject, we will turn our steps toward the foundry, or casting shop.

This is an extensive building, where many men are employed. When we enter, we are almost stifled by the heat from the furnaces and the sulphurous fumes of the liquid mass of mingled copper and spelter, forming brass, which is glowing and seething in black-lead crucibles that are placed in the midst of fiery anthracite. We think of Shadrach, Meshach and Abednego, and shudder involuntarily as we shield our eyes from the scorching rays. But let us hurry through here, and explore some more agreeable branch of the establishment.

Each caster works at a wooden trough about eight feet long, thirty inches wide and twenty inches deep. Into this trough he carefully sieves prepared sand, slightly moistened. His first step is to place across the trough a planed board, about two feet long and sixteen inches wide. Upon this an iron frame, being one half of what is technically called a "flask," is placed. This frame has a depth of about two and a half inches. Within this, and upon the board, are arranged the brass patterns to be re-produced. Upon these is dusted, or sieved, a coating of fine facing-sand. The frame is then rapidly filled up from the trough. By a light bound the workman springs from the ground upon the sand, which he thus presses compactly into the frame until a solid mass is formed. The top is then smoothed off, and a board, similar to the lower one, is placed upon it, and the frame is reversed. The board that had been the lower one is removed, revealing the pattern imbedded in the sand. The other section of the frame or flask, is fitted in its place, and filled up as its fellow. The two are then separated, the patterns are carefully

removed, and grooves or gates are made in the sand.
The flasks are then re-united and firmly fastened
together by means of screws or clamps, and ranged
along with the open side upward. We are careful
now to keep to the windward of the furnaces, while
the caster by means of long tongs, takes out a cruci-
ble of molten brass and pours the fiery liquid into
the "gates" which lead into the mould. A few mo-
ments are sufficient to chill the metal in the "flask;"
the clamps are removed, and the sand is shaken out.
The casting is found complete, with the exception of
some fragments of brass which cling around the edges.
It is a matter of surprise to see how faithfully the finest
chased work has been transferred from the original
pattern to the copy.

While these castings are being removed to the filing-
shop, we will step outside into a cooler atmosphere.
We learn now that the high chimneys of the foundry
enable the workmen to dispense with bellows. These
immense conical structures create a great draught. In
the yard we find unmistakable evidences of the habitual
proximity of fire. Here are half-burnt clamps, and
black-lead crucibles fairly melted and glazed with the
intensity of the heat to which they have been subjected.
Here, too, are ruined tools, bent, scorched and rendered
useless by the action of the fierce caloric. In one
corner we find a fair representative of a Californian or
Australian gold-hunter. Our digger, like his distant
prototype, has selected a running stream for the scene
of his operations. A hydrant furnishes him with this
desideratum; a pick, a shovel, and a few sieves, some
coarser and others finer, are his tools; a heap of cinders,

ashes and other refuse from the foundry, is the auriferous soil from which he each month washes a large quantity of valuable metal.   The gold-hunter in the wilds of the American and British Ophirs took the hint from our patient delver for bits of metal, who washed brass before gold was thought of in connection with California.

There is no difficulty experienced in finding the whereabouts of the filing-room.   The incessant grating of scores of files creates a din that would guide a blind man to the spot.   Here the castings are conveyed from the foundry.   They are first "edged up" with coarse rasps, and then finished smoothly with finer tools.   In many instances a number of castings have to be joined together to form one piece.   When this is the case, the several component parts are conveyed to the soldering-room, where they are carefully fitted together, taking care to leave one edge more prominent than the other, the sections are then put into their proper places, and retained there by wrapping them with iron wire.   Particles of brass solder, which look like brazen saw-dust, are mingled with water and nicely applied along the projecting edge of the section.   The entire piece is then placed in a furnace where the solder is melted.   The work has, of course, to go through another filing after that process is finished.   The joints must be made with a great deal of care, or in gas fixtures the subtle fluid would make its escape through any tiny opening left by the workman.

Before the castings leave the filing and soldering-rooms, there is frequently much to be done in the way of turning and twisting of branches, crumpling of leaves, drilling holes, &c., &c.   The articles are then sent to

the dipping rooms, whither we will now wend our way.
Here a strong smell of acids is very perceptible, and
renders a visit so unpleasant as to cause us to hurry
through this department as rapidly as is consistent
with our determination to inspect thoroughly every
thing that is curious.

The various processes through which the articles pass
in this department are exceedingly curious and interesting.　Here every thing is done by chemical agents.
There are ranges of monstrous stone jars filled with
divers-colored acids of different degrees of strength;
pans and kettles are teeming with very suspicious-look-
ing liquids; and water, hot, milk warm, and perfectly
cold, is flowing copiously.　In fact, we have here a per-
fect laboratory.　When the brass comes out of the hands
of the filers, it is dirty and discolored, and has more or
less sand, or other foreign matter, clinging to it.　The
first act of the dipper is to take hold of the brazen
article with a pair of tongs and dip it into a jar of acid;
a moment only is required by this process to remove
every particle of dirt and soil from the surface; the
hungry chemical eats it off, and would soon devour the
brass itself if sufficient time was given it.　The dipper
will not suffer that, though, and he speedily takes out
the cleansed metal and places it into water, which forth-
with washes off the acid and puts a stop to its ravages.
This first operation is called "pickling."　The color is
then essentially brass-like, as the "pickle" has devoured
every extraneous substance from the surface.　The article (say a girandole) which is undergoing the cleansing
process is then dipped into another jar, the contents of
which are a mystery to us.　This has the effect to

render the surface a rich sulphur color.   This operation occupies but a moment; the girandole is again washed in clean water, and then plunged into a chemical combination called an ormolu; in a few minutes the color of the metal is changed to a dirty yellow.   The ormolu is then washed off, and the surface of the girandole is found, upon close inspection, to have been eaten into minute molecules by the ravenous ormolu.   One more dip into an acid which makes the brass a rich, pale gold color, finishes the chemical ordeal.   After the girandole is cleansed in water, it presents a rich and uniform, though dull gold color.   This dulness forms a good foil, and contrasts handsomely with the prominent parts of the design, which are afterwards richly burnished, the ormolu having prepared the surface of the metal for that operation.   Before going to the burnishing-room, we will step into an apartment which adjoins that of the dipper, and witness the transformation of brass into silver.   This curious operation is performed by means of the galvanic battery.   The girandole, whose progress we have watched with much interest, is now connected with a wire leading from the galvanic battery, and is made to form the negative pole of the instrument.   The operator then takes a bar of pure silver, which acts as the positive pole of the battery.   The girandole is then held in a solution and the bar of silver played around it under the surface for a few seconds, which suffices to precipitate upon the ormolu'd brass a coat of the precious metal sufficiently thick to bear without injury the action of the burnishing instruments.   This process is exceedingly curious and interesting.   Before leaving the dipping-room, we must make some inquiries concerning the effect the chemicals exercise on the health of those who work among them. We are informed that a Hercules, with whom we have been chatting, has been among the acids for many years. He now weighs somewhere in the vicinity of two hundred pounds. If the drugs poison the air, our worthy dipper must be some kin to old King Mithridates, who is said to have lived and grown fat on poisons. But we prefer a purer atmosphere, so we will take leave of the dippers and their chemical wonders.

There is a little army of hands employed in the burnishing-room. The tools used here are of a great variety of shapes; they are formed either of highly-polished steel or a very hard material called blood-stone. The prominent parts of the work are highly polished by means of these burnishing tools, which are dipped freely into a dark-colored liquid. Thoughts of deadly poisons again take posession of our mind, but we experience much relief on being assured that the mysterious chemical is nothing more than small beer! —less it could not conveniently be. The parts of the surface of the metal which are not burnished are left "dead" or "matted," as they came from the ormolu. Burnishing is an important process. Much of the beauty and character of the work depends upon a judicious selection of the parts to be brought out by the burnisher. It is to the proper development of the design, what lights and shades are to a good picture. After the brass is burnished it is again cleansed by means of acids, and finally washed in hot water, the heat of which soon causes the work to dry: it is then thrown into a trough containing bookbinder's paper-shavings, which completes the drying. The work is now ready for lacquering.

While in the burnishing-rooms we were inclined to become believers in the story of Aladdin's wonderful lamp. The fiction goes that Aladdin had only to rub a lamp to have all his wants supplied. Here dozens of men with their families are furnished with food and raiment in precisely the same way. The lacquering room, is a very uncomfortable place in hot weather, being liberally supplied with stoves, which are kept constantly heated. Here the various pieces are taken from their paper bed and placed upon the hot iron, after being carefully brushed. When heated to a certain degree, the articles are taken (by means of proper instruments,) to a table, where the lacquer is applied with flat brushes made of camel's hair. The lacquer is composed of a certain gum dissolved in alcohol. Some articles are dipped into the lacquer, and "slung" backwards and forwards to insure its being properly spread over their surface. The lacquering is of the utmost importance, and requires the lacquer to be scientifically made and skilfully applied to ensure a rich and lasting gold color, unaffected by the action of the atmosphere.

The different parts and ornaments are now ready to be placed in the hands of the fitter, or finisher, and are therefore selected and carried to the respective places arranged for putting them together. One room is occupied entirely by a number of men who are constantly employed in fitting together such gas work as chandeliers, pendants, brackets, &c.; another to girandoles and candelabras; and a third to the numerous class

2

of solar lamps designed for standing upon the table, or for being suspended from the ceiling or against the wall. From all these apartments the goods are taken to meet once more in the packing-room previous to bidding a final farewell to their birth-place.

Some of the ornamental work is painted in parti-colors to please fanciful tastes; some is bronzed with different shades; while other work is covered with a coating of fine gold, or tastefully enameled.

We have now traced the various processes by which blocks of spelter and ingots of copper are converted into beautifully-formed and elaborately-ornamented arti-cles of use and taste. But many of these ornaments are only the branches, the outer flourishes of a grand design. To describe the construction of a chandelier, we must retrace our steps.

The main body of a chandelier is formed of a hollow shell of brass, technically called a "bowl." In former days the making of these bowls was a laborious and tedious operation. A plate of brass had to be hammered into shape by hand. This process often occupied eight or nine hours; now by means of the improved machinery which Messrs. Cornelius & Baker have in use, a man will turn out some dozen in a day.

We will attempt to describe the operation. A plate of brass is first cut into a circular form by an ingeniously-contrived machine. This round plate has a hole cut in its centre; it is then taken to a turning lathe; a block of wood of the desired patten is placed firmly upon the lathe, and the brass plate before described is secured by its centre to the wooden form. The "spinner" then lubricates the surface of the plate to make his tools work easily. The lathe is set in motion, and the wooden block, with the brass plate attached, is made to revolve rapidly ; the spinner, then by means of a smooth iron tool which has a long wooden handle, presses the plate over the wooden mould until it covers closely every part of the pattern. This forms a "bowl" of any shape which may be desired. The process is expeditious, but it requires great manual strength in the operator, and is fraught with infinite danger to his fingers, which are frequently brought into an uncomfortably close contact with the ragged edge of a brass plate revolving at a furious speed. A circular saw would not amputate a finger with more certainty if the endangered digit should come in its way. These bowls, after being "spun," are soldered together at the edges, and after going through the process of turning, filing, fitting, dipping, burnishing and lacquering, before described, they are, made to form the main body or centre of the chandelier, upon which the branches ornaments, &c., are securely fastened by means of screws. Vases, and a variety of other articles, are "spun" in the same manner, and pass through the same formula before making their appearance in the show-room.

We have been much bewildered in many rooms through which we have passed at witnessing the world of lathes, straps and wheels, which were creaking whirling and groaning about us, all impelled by the giant arm of steam. There is a vast deal of turning of metals required in the prosecution of this immense business. The drilling-machines, tapping-machines and screw-cutters would of themselves form the subject of a long article. Many hands are constantly employed cutting screws. This is done very expeditiously. Great care and skill is requisite in this branch. All the screws of the different classes that are turned out of this establishment are made of one size. If the branch of a chandelier exported by this house to China should find its way to Russia, it would fit exactly into any of the chandeliers in the Kremlin. This screw-cutting is a nice operation, and requires great skill in the cutter, as his work must fit so as to be perfectly air-tight.

The manufacture of gas burners is an important feature. These articles are exposed to a great heat when in use, and consequently have to be made of hard cast-iron. The burner is moulded in a solid form ; from the caster it goes into the hands of the filer, who "roughs" it off. The next operation is to drill it, to make it hollow. This we fancied must be a very tedious and toilsome task, but we were pleasantly surprised to see the drill scoop out the hard iron with the same facility as if it had been rich old cheese. The turning lathe and the finely-tempered drills made nothing of this operation, but chipped out the hard cast-iron as though the employment was rather agreeable than otherwise. The burner has then to go into the hands of the turner, who quickly removes the superfluous iron from the outside, and generally puts a tasty finish upon the article. The burner now looks like an iron ferrule. Before it can be made available for its legitimate use, it must be "tapped" so as to screw on the brass fixtures. It has also to be drilled with two tiny holes if intended, for a "fishtail" burner, or have a fine slit sawed in the end if designed for a "bat-wing." Both these operations require great skill and caution in the workman. The burner, after this has been performed, is to be polished, and it is then ready for use.

There are other rooms appropriated to glass cutting, grinding and polishing, which are done entirely by steam. We enter one apartment in which great numbers of men are employed in making the keys or faucets of the gas fixtures. They must be made to operate with safety and certainty. This work requires a great deal of care, as an aperture the size of a pin's point would be considered a serious leak. To insure a close fit, each key and its appropriate socket is ground out with emery. There are eighteen men constantly employed at this seemingly trifling branch of grinding keys. There are other places in which tin and coppersmiths are engaged at their peculiar branches of the business. The operations here are too familiar to the reader to render a description interesting.

There are rooms appropriated to the workers in artistic bronze, others, occupied by those who are employed at "damask" work. The "damask" is done with lacquer and acids. The candelabras, girandoles, standing solar lamps, and many other articles, are made with a marble base. There is a shop where a number of men are employed cutting and polishing the marble for this branch. We must inspect the enameling on glass, as the operation is exceedingly curious and tasteful. The operator here is an artist. He first makes a sketch on drawing-paper, of the design he intends enameling. The glass on which the painting is to be made, is then laid flat upon the drawing. The artist then paints the outlines on the back of the glass. The view to be transferred is perhaps a moonlight scene, with a castle and a bridge, and other pretty etceteras. A piece of stout paper is fitted to the shape of the glass ; on this, bits of mother-of-pearl are affixed here and there. The artist puts a small piece on the spot where the moon will come on the picture; another, and a larger piece is placed opposite the bridge, and a still larger portion where it will represent the castle. The artist then paints the glass around these objects to suit his taste, taking care that the colors shall be opaque. The glass, within the space allotted for the bridge, and the castle, is shaded, and the necessary windows, &c., are painted there in outline. A clean circular space is left on the glass for the moon. After the painting is finished the glass is secured to the paper back on which the bits of pearl have been attached, and an exquisite picture, with the most conspicuous objects in mother-of-pearl, produced. One of these enameled views is put into a handsome brass frame, and forms the centre of a girandole, or a bracket, which would do no discredit to the most elegant drawing-room.

We will pass through the packing-rooms before leaving the establishment, where men are constantly engaged at papering and packing to fill orders for all parts of the world. Tons of paper are used here annually, and several carpenters are busy manufacturing packing-boxes in which to transport the goods.

Before leaving, we will step into the "Museum." This is a large and well-stocked room, that is kept under lock and key, and watched with jealous care. Here a copy is preserved of every pattern made by the proprietors since the commencement. Almost every-thing worthy of being copied has its effigy or counter-

part in this room.   The collection is valued at a high
rate, the articles could not be replaced.   The " Museum"
contains many beautiful gems of the pattern-maker's art.
We are loth to leave this spot, but time passes.

There is a large basement fitted up with bins, in which
the articles are temporarily placed while waiting to be
shipped.   Each bin is marked with the name of the
place to which its contents are to be sent.   Among them
we noticed China, India, various ports in South America,
Havana, and the Canadas.

We are now through our explorations.   The variety of
branches of art and mechanism carried on in this establishment, has compelled us to merely glance over many
matters that are worthy of more critical examination.
The din of machinery, its intricate and complicated
character, the varied operations of its many busy hands,
and the strangeness of much that we saw, tended to
bewilder and puzzle our faculties.   We believe, though,
that we have given as good a description of the prominent features of the establishment as our allotted limits
will permit.   We feel confident that every one who
takes an interest in the advancement of the mechanic
arts, will feel an honest pride in the high character
which the products of this manufactory sustain for
themselves all over the world.

We believe all the various capitols of the United
States have been lighted by chandeliers manufactured
at this establishment.   The chandeliers and brackets
for the State Capitol at Columbus, Ohio, deserve a spe-
cial mention ; they were really the first pieces of work-
manship of the kind we ever saw ; prominent among
the embellishments, were beautiful statuettes of Pru-

dence, Science, Commerce, Liberty, America, and Simon Kenton; the latter in honor of the original settler of that State. These figures were modelled with great truthfulness to nature, and bronzed in the highest style of art. The American Eagle also, formed a conspicuous part in the ornamentation, with the stars suspended from his beak.

The chandeliers of the Hall of Representatives at Nashville, Tennessee, is a mammoth of its kind—it is fifteen feet in diameter; on it, and used as decorations, are buffaloes, Indians, corn, cotton, and tobacco plants, thus representing the products of the State in the last three mentioned articles.

The gas fixtures in the Academy of Music, at Philadelphia, were also made here. The chandelier hanging in the auditorium is said to be the largest in the world, being sixteen feet in diameter and twenty-five long, it has two hundred and forty burners, which, when lighted shed a sun-like brilliancy on all below. This firm has just finished the lighting apparatus for the House of Representatives at Washington, which is a great curiosity in itself. A pair of figures in bronze for sustaining the large clock in the same hall, are about being sent off to their destination, they represent an Indian and a Western hunter, each about three feet high, and we feel satisfied from a critical examination of them they could not be excelled in any part of the world.